DRIED
FLOWERS
FOR THE
HOME

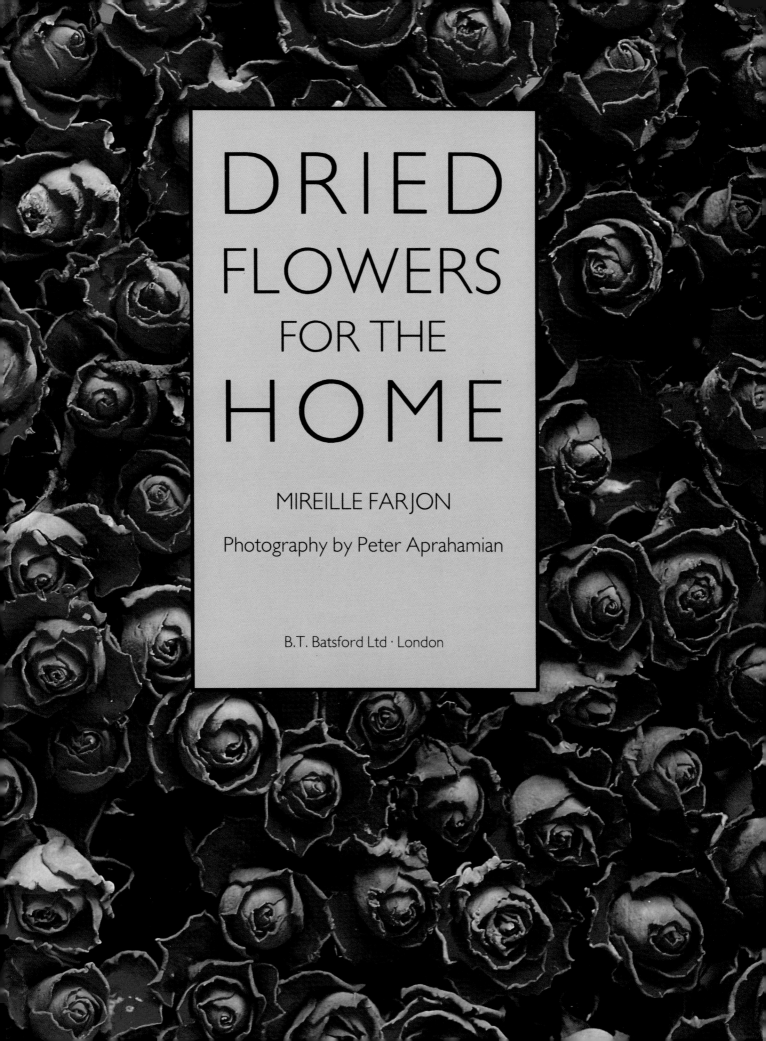

DRIED FLOWERS FOR THE HOME

MIREILLE FARJON

Photography by Peter Aprahamian

B.T. Batsford Ltd · London

For my mother,
for her unlimited and unconditional love

For Benjamin and Laura,
for giving me so much support and happiness

First published 1993

© Mireille Farjon, 1993

All photographs © Peter Aprahamian

Typeset by Goodfellow & Egan Ltd, Cambridge
and printed in Hong Kong

Published by
B.T. Batsford Ltd
4 Fitzhardinge Street
London W1H 0AH

A catalogue record for this book is available from the British
Library

ISBN 0 7134 7095 X

ACKNOWLEDGEMENTS

My particular thanks go to Samantha Stead, my editor, whose constant enthusiasm and encouragement have made this publication possible.

I would also like to thank: Peter Aprahamian for the wonderful photographs; Sue Lacey for the beautiful book design; Britannia Nurseries and Star Flowers for their contribution towards the flowers featured in the arrangements; Kenneth Turner, Lynne Lawrence and Ronaldo Maia for their valuable time, and all the other clients and private individuals who kindly agreed to be featured in this book, including:

The Royal Opera House, Covent Garden, London
Crabtree & Evelyn Ltd
Penhaligon's, Covent Garden, London
Jane Churchill Interiors Limited

The Draycott Hotel, London
Hotel De Crillon, Paris
Hotel Duc de Saint-Simon, Paris
Michael and Amanda Lakin
The Hon. Mrs J. Lakin
Lady Blakenham
Laurence Veillet-Lavallée
Linda Sullivan
Heather and Richard Kossow
Sarah Hutchinson
Guler Tunca
Sirin Edin
Helm Architects, Nick Helm
Anthea Franklin and Janie de Savary for their generous support, and many others.

CONTENTS

FOREWORD

My first encounter with dried flowers was purely accidental. It happened one afternoon when I returned late from France to England with my two children: the flowers on my table had been left for too long in their vase without any water, and were quite dry, but they had kept their natural colour perfectly and looked even more attractive dried than when fresh. In that moment I discovered the beauty of dried flowers, and from these few bunches left to dry inadvertently in the vase, I started to build my first arrangement. Gradually, as I came upon them, I added to these bunches more and more dried flowers of the same tone. As the arrangement grew, my friends began to comment on my apparent talent, and suggested that I go to look at the creations of the leading floral decorator, Kenneth Turner.

I followed my friends' advice, and was absolutely taken aback by the excellence of his work, which was a revelation to me of what could be achieved with dried flowers. This visit inspired me to carry on more seriously, and to work to find my own style in dried flower arranging. The only way to achieve this goal was to exercise my imagination by experimenting with the different flowers, textures, containers and interiors that my first commissions presented to me.

My strong passion for dried flowers has made me decide to write this book, to enable me to share my pleasure of working with them and to help you appreciate the often under-estimated beauty and potential of dried flowers. In so doing, I hope my book will thus become a tribute to those few flowers left to dry accidently in the vase, which have since brought so much excitement and happiness into my life, at a time when I needed it most.

A dried lotus flower is the queen of dried flowers: lotus flowers are dried naturally here, one with its petals unfolded and then refolded in half, in typical Thai fashion, and the other two with their petals wide open. The creamy colour of the lotus flowers offers a wonderful contrast to the green reindeer moss showing through the glass container

DRIED
FLOWERS
FOR INTERIORS

INTRODUCTION

A DRIED FLOWER AWAKENING

Once upon a time there was not a florist that did not have a display of dried flowers in the window, usually arranged in a fan shape and invariably consisting of rather unattractive brown and yellow flowers and foliage. They had little real appeal, because they looked so much more like dead flowers than dried. But about ten years ago, a big change began. Gradually, dried flowers started to become more sophisticated, and brighter, more natural colours started to come on to the market, and some results were so good that it became quite difficult to distinguish a dried flower from a fresh one, except to the touch. Then suddenly, dried flowers were everywhere: shop windows used them to enhance their products and florists started to work with them in a manner that had never been seen before. They were no longer content with poor quality, dead-looking dried flower arrangements, and in the hands of the best floral decorators grew floral creations that were worthy of the status of works of art.

A new era had begun and today people expect far more from dried flowers than the old brown and yellow fan-shaped arrangements: more varied and sophisticated compositions, as well as 'sculptured' dried flower arrangements, are among the many new popular ways of presenting dried materials.

The people more responsible than anyone else for revealing the tremendous beauty inherent in dried flowers and for showing what can be achieved with them, are a few pioneering floral designers whose work is a constant inspiration.

THE FLORAL DECORATORS

Ronaldo Maia, in New York, started working with flowers more than twenty years ago. He was one of the first artists to work with all floral media, fresh and dried, provided they were natural. His work brought him fame throughout the world and many artists have been influenced by his way of presenting flowers.

Meanwhile, in Copenhagen, another style was being developed by the floral artist Tage Andersen. Like Ronaldo Maia, Tage Andersen uses all types of media and assembles them into the most unusual shapes. His style is characterized by very voluptuous and extravagant designs. His book *Tage Andersen* (see Further Reading, page 124) is a fine example of what can be achieved with flowers, both fresh and dried.

More recently, in Paris, Jules des Prés was the first French floral design company to present us with the new look in dried flower arranging. Their symmetrical way of displaying roses, dahlias, herbs and grasses, in square or round baskets, symbolizes for me the Modernism in dried flower arranging, where symmetrical lines predominate.

Few dried flowers can surpass the rich beauty of dried roses. Against the sumptuous dark red wallpaper this arrangement is both highlighted in the candlelight, and reflects the colour scheme of this elegant dining-room, while its symmetrical style allows the full beauty of the container to be appreciated

Red and green are the main colours in this arrangement, chosen
both to blend with the silver-grey drapes, and to bring a little
more colour to the room by picking out the red in the pelmet.
Arranged in a fan shape, the red roses are inserted here and
there amongst the seed heads and foliage of amaranthus, palm
leaves, ruscus and eryngium. Lavender was later added to soften
the overall feel of the arrangement

It was important that the container did not detract from this
glorious arrangement, so as low a basket as possible, in as dark a
tone as possible, was used, and the flowers and foliage arranged
to hide much of it

In London, a similar style is seen in the extraordinary talent of the floral artist Kenneth Turner. The key to his consummate skill lies mainly in minute attention to detail, with nothing being left to chance. His shop is a perfect showcase of arrangements, dried or fresh, skilfully arranged en masse in most attractive containers: in his hands the flowers take the shape of sculptures that enhance the beauty of any interior.

Above: A stunning pair of vivid red topiary trees. Designed by Kenneth Turner

Right: This avant-garde dried flower arrangement illustrates the drastic change in our perception of the possibilities dried flowers offer: this modern sculpture is striking against the antique polished brass, yet does not jar

Above: When there is no time to arrange fresh flowers for the home for a special lunch or dinner party, your dried flower arrangement is the perfect compromise. The beeswax candles add a touch of elegance in this simple setting

Right: In this fan-shaped arrangement, where poplar leaves encircle the rim of the basket, flowers complement the colours found in the antique folding-screen: solidaster, roses, echinops, helichrysum, and astilbe are perfect here

Lavender, arranged in layers, adds style to any room. Here the dark blue of the lavender picks out the blue in the wallpaper (much less predominant than the red), in this room decorated by Jane Churchill Interiors Limited

Lynne Lawrence is another London designer who uses her imaginative talent to design flower arrangements for private homes or parties where creating the right mood is so important. When I first entered her shop, I was taken aback by a life-size kangaroo, made entirely with green moss! This epitomizes her artistic talent: anyone who wants a successful party could rest in peace after visiting her shop; every bunch of flowers has character, and the most common of them takes on an air of striking originality when arranged by her (see page 74).

Although the early 1980s saw a drastic change in the approach to arranging dried flowers, people witnessed this change in only very exclusive florists' shops. The high street look had still not changed much, and the same sad-looking dried flowers continued to be displayed. With so many more dried flowers on the market, you might have expected to find the most wonderful arrangements, but these things take time, and for one reason or another,

the same style seemed to continue: dead-looking flowers, arranged poorly, in equally unattractive containers. But now, the new look has arrived! Things have begun to change in the high street too and the old-style, dead-looking dried flower arrangements are gradually disappearing: more and more, people want new-style dried flowers in all colours to decorate their homes.

A dried flower arrangement can now be created to match the colour scheme in any room and in harmony with the atmosphere and style of the interior: in compact arrangements in attractive containers, in the shape of small trees, animals and any number of sculptured forms, in pictures, as accessories, in all sorts of styles, and no longer just in exclusive florists' shops. Dried flowers nowadays are true objects of decoration in any interior, and represent an artistic investment, rather than simply an alternative way of flowering a house with the same display, for years on end.

PLANNING A SUCCESSFUL ARRANGEMENT

It must be said that dried flowers are certainly not cheap to buy, and therefore if you decide to decorate your house with dried flowers you must be aware that you will need a great quantity of flowers to make a medium-size arrangement. However, if the arrangement proves successful, you will possess a display that will last for many years. Imagine all the fresh flowers you would have bought in that time and you will not regret having invested in your dried flower arrangement.

Although there is no strictly defined technique in the art of arranging dried flowers, it is not as easy as it seems to achieve good results, and planning your arrangements beforehand is absolutely vital. Lack of preparation is one of the most common reasons for failing to achieve what you hope for. However, if you follow certain golden rules from the start, it is possible to achieve very attractive results, and a wonderful display of dried flowers for any room in your home.

In planning your arrangement you should consider carefully the following factors: the style of the interior itself, including furnishings, wallpapers, fabrics and general atmosphere; the container; the style of the arrangement; the position of the arrangement, and especially its function in the room. Each of these factors is vitally important and if you ignore one of them your whole arrangement and its effect will suffer.

Inevitably, all these considerations are interlinked, and it is impossible to think of one without the other. Of course for the purposes of this book I have discussed them separately, but always bear in mind that they cannot be dissociated from one another.

THE STYLE OF THE INTERIOR AND CHOOSING A CONTAINER

Look closely at the room where the arrangement is going to be in order to decide on an appropriate style for your arrangement: for example, a restrained, symmetrical arrangement would fit quite well in a very sparse and modern room, but a large, traditional fan-shaped arrangement might be far too fussy and overwhelming. Always aim for a balance between the style of your arrangement and the style of your interior decoration: both must complement each other and never jar or fight against each other. Having said that, if, for example, your room is very simple and decorated with very few colours, you can use the dried flower arrangement as a means of bringing in lavish, bold or exciting colours that are not otherwise displayed in the room.

Using lavender as the main flower for this arrangement in an entrance hall not only creates a vivid and interesting splash of colour as soon as you enter the house but also gives out the most wonderful scent, which can be revived from time to time with a home fragrance spray. Fresh green moss surrounds the base of the lavender for colour contrast, and also to hide the floral foam

22

The dark orange of these air-dried roses blends well with the colour scheme in the room, the orange in the curtains and the rich dark brown wood. Arranged in a symmetrical style they have an air of extreme elegance

Left: Topiary trees made with various cereals, flowers or fruits are fun, and work well in a kitchen where they can be moved around freely and often

Above: Placing a dried flower arrangement effectively in a fireplace can be difficult, as it will be seen from above and side-on. Here the lavender, arranged en masse, is surrounded by over a hundred deep red roses, picking out the pink in the carpet

As for the container, it too should fit in with the style of your room. The shape, size, colour and texture of your container are all of vital importance. If, for instance, you have a very sparse, modern house, a rustic basket would almost certainly look out of place, though the same basket would probably be perfect in a country kitchen. The choice of the container can be determined by the style of the room: take into account the furniture, the material pattern and the colour scheme. You must decide whether you want the container to be noticeable in the room or to blend in with the decoration, depending on the effect you want to achieve. For instance, if the colour and patterns in the room are overpowering you may want the style and shape of your container to remain quite simple, or alternatively you may want it to be as loud as the decor.

Make sure the container is right for the style of arrangement, or alternatively, it may help to determine that style. If your container has some interesting features on it, or is decorated with a beautiful paint effect, it would be sad to hide it entirely with the dried flowers: in this case, a symmetrical design would be called for, where all the flowers are arranged in an upright position, with the stems and heads all gathered together, to enable you to see the attractive container. In order not to detract from the container, the arrangement would need to remain as simple as possible in its line and colours.

THE POSITION AND FUNCTION OF THE ARRANGEMENT

The position of a dried flower arrangement within a room is very important if you want to derive the most from it. First of all, I would not advise anyone to place a fresh flower display right next to a dried flower arrangement unless their colours are very contrasting: although on their own dried flowers can look very natural, fresh flowers in juxtaposition tend to make dried flowers look 'dead'.

The arrangement may be used as the main focal point in the room. For instance, when the materials of the curtains or furniture contain an interesting colour tone that is hardly noticeable, you can make this colour stand out dramatically by selecting it for your dried flowers: the whole room will then come together and the dried flower arrangement will add the final touch to your well thought-out decoration scheme.

Always think about how – from what angle – your arrangement will be seen. If you decide to display a dried flower arrangement in your fireplace, for example, bear in mind that it should be as attractive seen from the top as from the sides, that is, it will be looked at both when sitting or standing.

Dried flowers can be used to enhance an existing style or to create one. It seems a shame to use dried flower arrangements just to fill in a space. They are in themselves beautiful decorative pieces that enhance a well-planned room. Many arrangements lose much of their impact because people set them in fireplaces or on top of kitchen units for no real reason except on occasion to do no more than hide an unwanted feature in the room or to fill a void. Dried flowers have more aesthetic value than that: look upon them as the fine painting on the wall, or any valuable object carefully selected for your interior.

So it is that the motive behind your dried flower arrangement is often the key to its successful insertion in your skilfully decorated home. Dried flower arrangements may be impressive in halls and sitting-rooms, or decorative details in other rooms such as kitchen or bathrooms. Sculptured tree-shaped arrangements look particularly attractive there, and are more practical: they usually need to be able to be moved around freely in a room that is usually smaller than others.

Finally, dried flower arrangements can make the most wonderful presents: set in silver containers or china bowls they are beautiful ornaments; animals, like the moss bear on page 71, are a fun addition to any interior, and a gift of flowers can be dried and arranged to create a lasting memento.

Exclusively designed for the Draycott Hotel in London, this arrangement, although put together in a symmetrical style, conveys the image of a fresh flower arrangement because of the choice of flowers. The outside of the basket is covered with green moss and the flowers used are pink *Helipterum manglesii*, and *Limonium suworowii*, with ruscus foliage. The choice of flowers blends well with the rustic scenery in the painting above and the generally peaceful atmosphere of the hotel

Red roses, air-dried, are reminiscent of a special evening, and in
a miniature arrangement are perfect set amongst other
ornaments and trinkets in a bedroom, or anywhere

The curtains in the sitting room were the inspiration for this arrangement, made with layers of pink and burgundy air-dried paeonies. The effect here is true trompe l'oeil: the vivid colours and the delicate texture of the petals are as fresh as the fresh paeonies depicted in the curtain material

THE STYLE OF THE ARRANGEMENT AND THE FLOWERS

When you buy your dried flowers, make sure they are as beautiful as when they were fresh and that the colours are as close to their natural colour as possible. Also make sure that the flowers seem robust: you do not want them to fall apart when you start working with them (if you want to dry flowers yourself, see page 38). Bear in mind all the time that once your arrangement has been built and the flower stems cut to the exact size for your container, it is very difficult to remove any unwanted material from the arrangement without damaging some flowers. Therefore, it pays to be patient when preparing your container and to plan your particular design.

Once you have decided on the general style of your arrangement and the style of container, you can choose the colours of the flowers. You may decide to use a colour that blends in with the colour scheme of the room, or on a contrasting colour. If you want the arrangement to stand out it is better to choose the latter. If you wish the dried flower arrangement and your decoration to form a whole, use the same tones of colour for your dried flower arrangement as the tones of colour in the rooms. Try not to use more than two tones of colour for your arrangement unless you wish to create a country look. By using just one or two tones of colour you will tend to create a simpler, more elegant effect. The many types of green foliage can be used very successfully as a foil to the flowers: the green of the foliage against a one single colour of flowers creates a particularly stylish combination.

This simple and elegant symmetrical arrangement of cream roses echoes perfectly both the shape of the table, the pictures and the fireplace, and the colour of the walls and furnishings

BUYING THE FLOWERS

A dried flower arrangement can double in price depending on the materials you choose for it. Paeonies and roses, which I use quite a lot, are particularly expensive, but there are of course many other attractive flowers that will have the same effect in an interior. Achillea, limonium, dahlias and the many cereals can all make wonderful arrangements, in all possible sizes and shapes and at small cost. However, I love paeonies and roses because of the timeless beauty they manage to convey so well when captured in the prime of their bloom. It is almost impossible to say whether they are dried or fresh when used in arrangement. They are also particularly easy to work with, both when using them with their whole stem, and when working with just the heads.

The textures of flowers are an important consideration, both for their visual impact (thorny as opposed to delicate, for example) but also from a practical point of view. For instance, certain flowers are almost impossible to use to make sculptured arrangements because of their fragility and rather brittle nature. Yet flowers like achillea, roses, and paeonies are ideal for making sculptured arrangements because of their hard, compact heads.

It is always better to order more dried material than you really need, particularly if you are making a large arrangement (see, for example, page 82), so as not to run short of a certain type of flower while making the arrangement – always very irritating and a waste of time. Although in Part Two I give guidelines on the number of flowers you will need for each project, it is impossible to predict exactly because the size and shape of every flower is naturally different. Of course, if you order your flowers in greater quantity you should also obtain a better price from your stockist.

Finally, we have seen that all the decorative elements of your home are strongly linked to each other, and you must continue to take them into consideration now. The choice of a specific container has a practical as well as aesthetic effect, and may determine not only the colour of the flowers but also their texture and their make-up. For instance, a tall glass container will naturally call for long-stemmed flowers.

If you want to dry your own flowers, see page 38.

33

Above: A medium-sized topiary tree made entirely with roses, paeonies and carnations in the same colour tones, all air-dried. Set in a simple glass container, filled with the petals of the roses and the paeonies, this tree looks wonderful either on its own, or in another china container of interesting shape and colour

Right: This luxurious arrangement is very much in keeping with the sumptuous bathroom: arranged in a natural style, long-stemmed paeonies, roses, lavender, and small eryngium are the main flowers used. The green reindeer moss inside the glass container adds an extra colour contrast

The colours of these flowers are kept as subdued as possible to blend in well with the light-grey urn and white kitchen-dining room. The design of the arrangement deliberately recalls the motif on the urn. If the arrangement is well protected from the direct sunlight, it should last more than five years, like this one

LIGHTING

If you want to get the best, visually, from your dried flower arrangements, whatever style you have chosen, you must have an adequate form of lighting. In the evening, when the natural light starts fading away, a dried flower arrangement can lose at least 80 per cent of its vibrancy. A simple low-voltage spot light concealed in the ceiling above will light it perfectly, but a lamp or two strategically positioned close by will do just as well.

CARING FOR THE ARRANGEMENT

As dried flowers are expensive to buy, make sure you protect them at all times from direct sunlight. Dried flowers do keep their colours for many years, but will not if placed in very bright and sunny rooms.

I rarely have a problem with dust, but dried flowers can get dusty, and the only remedy for this is to use a hair-dryer from time to time on a cool setting, and *very gently* direct it towards the flowers that need it most. If possible, keep the arrangement in as dust-free an environment as possible.

Dried flowers such as lavender and roses have a wonderful scent when first displayed in the room but they tend to lose this scent quite rapidly. You can revive the perfume by spraying over the flowers some of your home fragrance scent.

CONCLUSION

Understanding the interplay between your dried flower arrangement and its location in the room, the choice of flowers and the container, their relationship with the style of interior decoration, and so on, is the key to planning a successful arrangement for your home. Dried flowers offer endless possibilities to an interior, and it is really up to you to create in your dried flower arrangement the look you wish to achieve for your own home. The second part of this book shows how to create certain different styles, natural, sculptured, modern, symmetrical and traditional, in all sizes, and you can use these as the basis for your own particular ideal dried flower arrangement.

Lavender, eryngium, echinops, anaphalis, helichrysum and verticordia form the main body of this large arrangement. The lavender is worked in a criss-cross fashion all around the display

DRYING FLOWERS

DRYING FLOWERS COMMERCIALLY

Although there have always been some dried flowers in florists' shops, some fifteen years ago, apart from a few grasses and some unattractive yellow and pink Helichrysum, the choice in dried flowers was indeed very limited. The large range of dried flowers you can now find on the market is mainly due to the work of major companies in Europe who have undertaken the task of drying all the plant materials florists require. One of these companies, Star Flowers of Holland, whose flowers are featured in this book, started by experimenting with drying materials in their loft. Then the demand for dried flowers increased dramatically, particularly for flowers that had kept their original colours, and as a result, Star Flowers now exports all over the world. The varying demands from different countries led them to export not only a wide variety of their home-grown flowers, but also to import unusual flowers from outside their own country, for drying and re-export. Dried flowers are now imported and exported all over the world and it is fairly easy to acquire many exotic and interesting varieties.

Long gone are the days when Star Flowers dried their own flowers in a loft, and like any other major company, Star Flowers signs contracts with growers for the number of bunches they must produce for them to respond to an ever-growing demand. It is an operation where every month of the year is carefully planned. Several hundreds of thousands of bunches of different flowers are dried a week in different drying rooms. The circulation of air is essential for the drying process, and for this particular purpose there is a multitude of ventilators and heaters, and the moist air is sucked away as the warm dry air is blown in. After the drying process all the different flowers are allowed to breathe for a day so that the stems regain their flexibility. After that the dried flowers are ready to be dispatched worldwide, to the many countries where dried flowers have become more and more popular.

DRYING FLOWERS YOURSELF

It is possible to buy almost any ready-dried materials but I find that when you are arranging on a small scale it is very satisfactory to dry your own materials. There are many ways to dry flowers or leaves, but here are the two most commonly used methods, which are easy to carry out in your own home.

The flowers must be almost in bloom, but not too wide open, or their petals would fall off when drying.

Dark furniture and a predominance of antiquarian books suggested a darker colour tone for this arrangement, with touches of deep-coloured flowers and almost-golden leaves reflecting the beautiful book bindings. The branches in the centre were simply collected along the banks of the river. The flowers are dark burgundy roses and lavender, with artichokes, cedar cones, and rust and wine anthurium leaves

AIR-DRYING

This is the most commonly known method and the easiest. You will need a dark confined space, where the temperature level is constant, somewhere between 12°C and 15°C. An airing cupboard is ideal.

1. Select all the flowers that are ready to be dried; they should be not quite in full bloom.

2. Take some of the leaves near the heads off the stems (in doing so you prevent the heads from rotting, since the leaves clustered around them retain too much humidity).

3. Arrange them in bunches of five or six, heads against heads, and tie them all together with a piece of wire or string twisted around their stems, leaving a long enough end to hang them.

4. Hang them upside down to dry (preferably in an airing cupboard). The bunches must not touch each other, so that the air can circulate well around them.

5. In six or seven days your flowers should be dry, and should have retained their natural colours – although they do tend to go a tone darker. You can feel simply by touching whether your flowers have dried completely or not.

MOSS

You can buy moss ready-dried, but for sculptures it is easier and less expensive to use fresh moss, which is more malleable. The moss then dries on the sculpture quite naturally (it does not need to be placed in an airing cupboard), though it should be sprayed with water occasionally to keep it looking fresh and green.

USING SILICA GEL

Dessicants such as silica gel, which can be purchased from a chemist or drugstore, absorb the water contained in the flowers or leaves you wish to dry. Dried by this method, plant materials look very much like when they were fresh in both shape and colour. Silica gel consists of crystals that can be used over and over again. When handling it it is preferable to wear a mask to prevent you from inhaling toxic fumes. Silica gel is available with a colour indicator: the crystals are blue when you purchase them and turn pink when they have absorbed the moisture from the materials you need to dry.

The crystals need to be ground down to at least half their original size (you can use a mortar and pestle or an electric grinder) so that they cover all the plant materials fully. Choose an air-tight container.

1. Place a layer of the finely ground crystals in the air-tight container.

2. Lay the heads of the flowers or leaves on top of the crystals and cover them with the rest of the crystals until they are totally buried.

3. Close the container and make sure it is properly sealed.

4. After two or three days your materials should be ready to come out of the container. By now the colour indicator should have turned pink (if not, leave them a little longer). Remove your plant materials as soon as they are ready, since they will become brittle if you leave them for too long under the crystals.

5. To re-use the crystals simply place them on a shallow tray and put them in a warm oven. They will eventually turn blue as they dry out and will be ready to use again. Store them in an air-tight container.

A 'mushroom' tree made entirely with two sorts of moss (sphagnum moss for the tree-top and bun moss for the base). Ideal for a conservatory

TOOLS

To work with dried flowers you will need these essential tools and materials:

A pair of good florists' scissors
A pair of secateurs
Wire cutters
Dry floral foam in various shapes
Stub wires in various sizes and thicknesses
A good-length sharp knife
A pair of old leather gloves
A glue gun, or fairly strong household adhesive
A brush to clear away dust
Newspaper, or a large sheet to work on

For sculptures, in addition:
Chicken wire
Plaster of Paris
A stapler

MAKING THE
ARRANGEMENT

If at all possible it is far better to make the arrangement as close as possible to the place where it is going to stay, because first of all dried flowers are quite fragile to move (particularly if the arrangement is large), and second they create a lot of dust when you work with them. Of course it is also far better to work on site because all the factors of decoration which will affect the size and proportions of the arrangement are around you. Once you have decided on the style of your arrangement, lay a large sheet on the surface where you will be making the arrangement and lay all the flowers and foliage you will be using on top of it, grouped according to their colour tones. Now take each individual group of flowers and foliage and prepare them according to the sort of arrangement you are making (see Part Two). It is much easier to prepare all foliage and flowers before you start making the arrangement so that you have everything to hand.

Once everything is prepared, including your container, you are ready to begin. I like to think of creating a dried flower arrangement as though I were painting a picture and experimenting with colours, using deep, richly coloured flowers for shadows and lighter, more delicate flowers for highlights. Always beware of overdoing the colour: when I made my first arrangement I was so carried away by my enthusiasm for a particular yellow flower, I insisted on adding it to my predominately pink arrangement, despite the fact that the tone was all wrong. Of course it ruined the overall effect of the arrangement. When, in my disappointment, I tried to remove the yellow flowers, I discovered that removing dried materials is almost impossible without damaging them and the surrounding flowers – and creating a lot of mess!

So, always think very carefully about how you want your arrangement to look, and beware of getting over-excited. If you do make a mistake, do not despair, because it is not the end of the world – simply try to pull the flowers out at the same angle you put them in, and be very careful and gentle when you remove the materials.

Lavender is arranged here en masse at the top of the arrangement, surrounded by *Rosa* 'Paso Doble'; on each corner of the wire basket paeonies (dried using silica gel), are interspersed with magnolia leaves. The basket is lined with moss to hide the floral foam at the bottom of the arrangement. The pink in the large paeonies and the roses picks out the colour in the furnishings and forms a contrast with the strong green found in the paintings on the walls

ACHIEVING A SPECIFIC LOOK
FOR YOUR HOME

A NATURAL
STYLE

A 60 × 60 cm (23 × 23 in) arrangement of roses, paeonies, delphiniums and ruscus for the General Director's private room, the Royal Opera House, Covent Garden. Each individual flower is placed in the arrangement as if it were fresh, to create a sumptuous centrepiece that looks as natural as possible, and offsets dramatically the turquoise colour of the wallpaper.

MATERIALS

One plain glass container, round or square,
    approximately 15 × 15 cm (6 × 6 in)
One block of dry floral foam
One small plastic carrier bag, with no holes
Plaster of Paris
Plastic bowl for mixing the plaster
Stub wire

FLOWERS AND FOLIAGE

15 pink paeony heads (dried with silica gel)
40 pink paeonies (air-dried)
10 bunches Rosa 'Motrea'
 5 bunches Rosa 'Gerda'
 5 bunches pink delphiniums
 6 bunches Ruscus aculeatus (butcher's broom)
Rose leaves

THE LOCATION

Fan-shaped arrangements tend by their nature to imitate the natural look of fresh flowers, and the beauty of the dried flowers is often conveyed more effectively by larger-sized arrangements. These can look particularly stunning in hallways and drawing rooms, and always attract attention.

When I first entered this reception room, I was confronted by the arresting turquoise colour of the walls. The drapes over the table added an interesting mixture of deep yellow and burgundy. Otherwise, there was very little furniture indeed.

I decided to choose flowers that would contrast radically with the turquoise walls. Because the room was furnished so barely, and because turquoise is rather a cold colour, I felt that the room needed an arrangement that would both stand out and create warmth: hence I chose rich green foliage and a range of pink flowers with colours of varying depth.

THE CONTAINER

So it would not detract from the arrangement, I wanted the container to be hardly noticeable. Equally, I wanted to use as much of the warm colours of the flowers as possible. A plain glass container was the ideal answer, because it allowed me to display the flowers through the container as well as in the arrangement itself.

MAKING THE ARRANGEMENT

PREPARING THE CONTAINER

Paeony heads dried in silica gel retain both their volume and colour, and were therefore the best sort to use for lining the sides of the container, mixed with some green rose leaves. Lining the container takes a little patience, but I find this is the best method for securing them:

First mix enough Plaster of Paris in a plastic bowl to fill about half of the glass container. Make sure it is a fairly thick consistency.

Now balance the paeony heads against the sides of the container, placing a few rose leaves amongst them. Then, keeping hold of the flowers, carefully insert the small plastic carrier bag in the middle of the bowl, and gently press it against the flowers, which will keep the flower heads balanced for the moment. Leave the top of the plastic bag overlapping the sides of the container to protect the container and the flowers.

Make a final check to ensure that the plastic bag has no holes, and then carefully pour in the Plaster of Paris until the bag is about half full. Now take the block of foam (cut it to size if necessary) and insert it in the Plaster of Paris, leaving at least one third of its length exposed above the glass container. It is this exposed foam you will use for making the arrangement.

Once the Plaster of Paris has hardened, cut away the plastic bag so that nothing shows above the container. The plastic bag will press naturally against the sides of the container, securing the flower heads against its sides.

ARRANGING THE FLOWERS

You can create a 'natural' look with dried flowers simply by placing the flowers in their container, or in foam, as if

Pink flowers with long stems, mixed with green foliage, offset dramatically the turquoise colour of the wallpaper; the arrangement is designed to look as natural as possible and each individual flower is placed in the arrangement as if it were fresh, creating a fan shape. Ruscus foliage is used to form a knot around the rim of the glass container as a final decorative touch, and also to hide unwanted features such as wires and floral foam

they were fresh flowers. Your dried flower arrangement should then convey the same lightness and fluidity as a fresh flower display.

The first thing to do is to get a sense of the shape of your arrangement. Here I started with the green ruscus foliage, using it to create the basic outline, in the size I felt was required for the room. (It is difficult to be completely precise about this – every room and every situation will require something different, and you will need to use your own judgement.)

It is worth keeping one or two bunches of foliage aside for when you come to finish the arrangement.

Once all the foliage is in place, you can begin to position the roses. I kept them all in bunches of about eight or ten, rather than singling them out, so that the arrangement looked rather like an abstract painting, with patches of colour dotted all over.

Once all the roses were in position I added the paeonies, ensuring that they would not be hidden by other flowers. Again I positioned them asymmetrically, keeping some stems long and cutting others short, to give texture to the arrangement. As with the roses, I wanted the paeonies to give the impression of thick, voluptuous flower heads when viewed from a distance, and so kept these in bunches of three, tying the stems together with florist wire.

Finally I added the pink delphiniums, dividing the bunches in half this time. They were a much lighter pink, and so I placed them close to the paeonies to bring in some highlights.

You may find, as I did, that some of the stems are particularly fragile, and if so you will need to wire the stems with stub wire, wrapping it around each stem near the top and using the wire itself like a stem to secure the flower in the foam.

Once all the flowers are in place, you will find that there is an empty space around the rim of the container, and that some stems may be showing. In order to hide them and to fill the space, take the bunch of foliage you have kept aside and twist it very loosely around the rim of the container, encircling it twice, using one or two stems at a time. Make a knot at the end to stop the stems unwinding, and repeat with all the stems until all the space above the rim of the container is filled. You can make a final little knot with some florist wire to secure the stems completely.

Finally, I added some greenery at the base of the arrangement, which not only added fluidity but made the paeony heads inside the glass container stand out dramatically: the finishing touch.

Filling a glass container with flowers and foliage can also offset a sculptured arrangement as beautifully as a natural style one

A SCULPTURED TOPIARY TREE

A 105 × 60 cm (41 × 23 in) topiary tree, sculptured entirely with preserved magnolia leaves, for a high alcove in a passageway. The white antique milk pot makes a striking contrast with the almost black magnolia leaves; at the same time the soft lighting brings out the myriad shades of green in the leaves, allowing maximum interplay of light and texture.

MATERIALS

Two bunches of stub wire, medium or heavy
    gauge
Ten blocks of dry floral foam
Chicken wire, large enough to cover the top
    surface of the dry foam
One plastic carrier bag, with no holes
Plaster of Paris
A glue gun, or any strong adhesive
Florist's wire
A heavy stapler

FLOWERS AND FOLIAGE

Two large bags of preserved magnolia leaves
One small log or branch cut to size for the trunk
    (obtainable from a flower market)
Six or seven pieces of bun moss (*Grimmia
    pulvinata*)

THE LOCATION

It can be difficult to decorate a country house with dried flowers, especially if the house already uses all the cut flowers found in the garden to decorate the rooms. The particular location for this arrangement was extremely awkward, being an alcove above a kitchen door, whose height and lack of light made it almost impossible for fresh flowers to survive there for more than a day. A sculptured arrangement made with dried flowers was thus ideal for this empty space above the doorway. I decided to use magnolia leaves (which can be purchased from flower markets or ordered from florists in large bags – all the leaves preserved in glycerine) to make a topiary tree set in a white antique milk pot. The almost-black leaves and the whiteness of the milk pot created a striking contrast.

A small low voltage spotlight was later installed in the ceiling here to provide soft lighting – good lighting is very important for this sort of arangement to bring out all the textures and interesting shades of green in the leaves. Positioning lamps close by would create a similar effect.

The different shades of green found in the magnolia leaves and the lime green colour of the moss worked particularly well against the very pale pink painted wall of this elegant house in the country.

THE CONTAINER

On this occasion, I was given an antique milk pot to work with, but you can use any other type of container equally well. Make sure the size of the container is in proportion with the tree (here the container is 28 cm high or 10 inches).

MAKING THE ARRANGEMENT

PREPARING THE CONTAINER

Prepare the container as on page 50, by filling a plastic bag, inside the container, with Plaster of Paris. If you are using an old container and are worried about breaking it, make sure you line the sides of the container with some thin layers of dry foam before placing the plastic bag inside.

Place the plastic bag in the container, covering the rim with the top of the plastic bag to protect it from any spillage. Make sure the thin layers of dry foam remain in place while you pour in the Plaster of Paris, so that once it has set, the pressure of the plaster will be exercised on the dry foam and not on the sides of the container: the foam will effectively act as a cushion.

Keep your small log close to hand, so that when you have poured the Plaster of Paris into the container, to approximately half way up, you can place the tree trunk in the centre of the mixture. Wait for the plaster to harden enough so you can let go of the trunk without it falling over.

Once the trunk is secure in its upright position, cut away the edge of the plastic bag with a pair of scissors, until the bag is invisible inside the container.

MAKING THE TREE-TOP

For small or miniature trees (see page 60) you can buy spheres of dry foam to use as the base for your tree-top.

However, with a large arrangement like this you need to build up your own tree-top shape from blocks of foam. Cut the blocks down, if necessary, to the size you need for your sphere, gathering the blocks of foam all around the tree trunk at the top to form a rough tree-top shape. Secure them with the glue gun. The tree need not be perfectly spherical, but cut off any corners that jut out too far so that you do have a basic rounded form to work with.

Since magnolia leaves are quite long (about 19 cm (7 in)), make sure that the sphere of dry foam is not too large to begin with, so that once the leaves are in position, the tree top will not look top-heavy and out of proportion with the container and the tree trunk.

Using the glue gun, secure the blocks of dry foam around the top of the tree trunk to form a round-shaped ball. Now use some florist wire to bind the pieces of dry foam together so that they do not slip off the top of the trunk.

Once the dry foam is firmly in place and you are satisfied with its shape, use the chicken wire to cover the dry foam, pressing it down firmly. Use a heavy stapler to secure the chicken wire to the trunk, as close as possible to the dry foam, so that once the tree is finished you will not be able to see either the chicken wire or the staples. All this will eventually be hidden under the leaves. The chicken wire must cover all the dry foam so that the top of the tree remains firmly secured to the tree trunk and does not move about. Once you are satisfied that you have achieved this successfully you can prepare all the magnolia leaves.

You will need to wire each individual leaf simply by inserting a stub wire into the base of the leaf, where the stem begins, and winding the rest of the wire around the top of the stem. Alternatively, if you think you have made the foam base of the tree-top too small, you can use the leaves as a guideline and the stub wire as the extra length required to make the tree larger at the top; insert however much wire you think necessary into the dry foam. The stub wire must be thick enough in this instance not to bend.

Now for patience – wiring all the magnolia leaves will take approximately three hours for the size of the tree featured here! Once you have finished all the wiring, you will then be able to start arranging the leaves on the tree-top.

Miniature topiary trees make a wonderful entrance to a doll's house; made with bupleurum, they are set in hand-made terracotta pots no taller than 7 cm (3 in)

ARRANGING THE LEAVES

Insert the leaves one by one into the dry foam, making sure all the time that you do not lose the shape you want for your tree. This is best achieved by using the first leaves to outline the shape – to act as markers. In this particular instance I wanted the tree to be quite round and so used some leaves as a guideline, placing them all around the tree very sparsely to start with, just to get an idea of the shape. I then worked round and round the tree methodically, and gradually the tree became denser as the leaves drew closer and closer together. Then, finally, there was no more room to insert more magnolia leaves.

As a final touch, I placed the bun moss around the base of the tree trunk to create the illusion of a tree planted in some mossy earth.

A MINIATURE ORNAMENTAL TREE

A 23 cm (9 in) miniature tree of delicate air-dried red roses looks exquisite set in an antique silver container finely engraved with flowers. A beautiful and precious ornament for any mantelpiece or dressing table, this rose tree is the perfect memento of a special evening. Miniature trees can be made with almost any flowers or foliage, for any container, and for any room.

MATERIALS

One small plastic bag to fit your container
Plaster of Paris
One small floral foam sphere
One small branch cut to the required length
Some stub wire
A glue gun or other adhesive

FLOWERS AND FOLIAGE

One handful of bun moss (*Grimmia pulvinata*) or
    reindeer moss (*Cladonia*)
Four or five bunches of roses in the colour of
    your choice

THE LOCATION

Set on any surface – a shelf, a small table, in a bathroom, in a bedroom – or simply as a present, miniature dried flower arrangements make beautiful, elegant ornaments, especially if arranged with the flower heads tight together, in a symmetrical fashion.

However small the arrangement, you will be surprised at the enormous quantity of flowers you need. But since the colour lasts for many years it is worth the investment in a few bunches of roses. I am particularly fond of small trees made entirely with rose buds. Equally, if you are privileged enough to be offered some roses in bloom, they are extremely easy to air dry, and arranged in the shape of a miniature tree, they become not only a beautiful ornament, but also a lasting memento.

THE CONTAINER

You can use any size of container in the style of your choice: tiny terracotta pots, for example, can look very attractive. On this particular occasion I chose an antique silver goblet, a christening present for one member of the family, in whose room the arrangement was to stay.

MAKING THE ARRANGEMENT

PREPARING THE CONTAINER

Whatever the size or style of your container, you must still follow the same careful preparatory procedure as before. If your container is made of a material like silver or any other metal it is not necessary to line the inside of the container with thin layers of dry foam, since the silver container is unlikely to break when the plaster expands as it sets. But, if your container is made of china, follow the procedure on page 56.

In this instance, you still need to use the plastic bag to line the container, both to protect the silver from any spillage of plaster and also to remove the arrangement more easily when in future years it begins to look tired and faded.

Take a small branch and cut it to the length you need for your miniature tree (you may want your own tree to be slightly shorter or taller than mine, depending on the

The delicate red roses are the perfect complement to the fine floral decoration on the silver container

These miniature trees in tiny terracotta pots, made for Crabtree & Evelyn, and reflecting their logo, blend well with the different soap figurines and would look very attractive in a children's bathroom or nursery

shape of the container), and pour the Plaster of Paris into the small plastic bag, filling it two-thirds of the way up. As soon as you have done that, place the small branch in position, to simulate a tree trunk in miniature size; let it go when you feel the plaster has set, which usually takes five minutes or so.

Once you are satisfied that the plaster has hardened, place the small sphere of dry foam on top of the branch by pressing it down firmly on top. Remove the small sphere, put some glue inside the hole you have created, and replace it, this time holding on for a few minutes until it is firmly glued to the branch.

ARRANGING THE FLOWERS

You can now prepare all the roses. Break all the rose heads from their stems, leaving at least two or three centimetres of stem attached. Use this part of the stem to stick the rose heads into the sphere, working round methodically until the dry sphere is totally covered with roses pressed hard head to head, forming a very compact ball.

Now cut away the plastic bag so that it does not show and is well tucked inside the container. Cover the base of the arrangement with some moss, leaving a little moss overlapping the container slightly if you prefer.

These arrangements are ideal presents for someone special and can look very attractive against a background of other precious ornaments and decorative objects in your home. You can also make balls of flowers in their own right (not attaching them to a tree), using flowers of different colours, or not if you prefer – these can look stunning on a dressing table.

A beautiful ball of dried roses in different shades of pink and red (made in the same way as a miniature tree-top) looks wonderful set against these elegant perfume bottles. Commissioned by Penhaligon's, London

A COUNTRY LOOK

A simple arrangement of cereal grasses, 40 × 58 cm (16 × 23 in), which brings a little corner of the wheat fields outside into the kitchen of an early nineteenth-century country house in the south-west of France. Dark green moss is laid around the rim of the rich blue enamel container: the combination of blue and green works perfectly to add a striking patch of colour in a room where white predominates.

MAKING THE ARRANGEMENT

PREPARING THE CONTAINER

Fill the container with the dry floral foam, pressing it against the sides of the bucket and binding all the blocks together with stub wire, to ensure that the dry foam will stay in position if the arrangement is moved. Once you are absolutely sure the blocks of dry foam are firmly in place (shake the container and see what happens: if the blocks move even slightly you must secure them better, by inserting small pieces of foam in the gaps found between the sides of the container and the pieces of foam), start by laying the freshly cut green wheat on the floor, and prepare small bunches of wheat at a time, by cutting them all to the same length. I chose for this arrangement the cereal that was grown in the fields surrounding this country house, and I simply judged roughly how much wheat I would need to cover the whole of the old blue enamel bowl.

ARRANGING THE GRASSES

I started by arranging the wheat at the centre of the container in a rather methodical way, all the stems upright and as tightly against one another as possible, in order to

---

> ### MATERIALS
>
> Six blocks of dry floral foam, or enough to fill
>   your container
> Some stub wire
> One low circular container of your choice
>
> ### FLOWERS AND FOLIAGE
>
> Seven bunches or so of green wheat
> Reindeer moss in a dark green colour

THE LOCATION

The symmetry found in this arrangement, coupled with the use of any type of cereal or grass you choose (for example oat grass (*Avena*), canary reed grass (*Phalaris*), brome grass (*Bromus*), wheat (*Triticum*) or barley (*Hordeum*)), means it can fit well in many styles of interior, whether modern or more traditional.

I wanted to bring into this French country kitchen a little piece of the wheat fields outside. To convey the impression of a small corner of the field brought into the house, I decided on a fairly symmetrical arrangement, where all the wheat would be arranged upright, packed together quite tightly, to recall the wheat growing in the field outside.

THE CONTAINER

For my arrangement I used an old, once discarded, blue enamel bowl. I particularly liked the rich blue enamel of the bowl, which formed a radical contrast with the fresh green colour of the wheat and moss. Again, you can use any suitable container.

Set against the wall, by the open shutters, the arrangement made with wheat recalls the cereal found in the fields outside. The pompon at its centre adds a little humour and relief to this rather severe symmetrical arrangement

This is one way of using up left-over flowers: a pretty wreath will last for a very long time, and can be placed on a door inside the house or simply on a mantlepiece. Blue and pink delphiniums are the only flowers used here, mixed with some wheat. I wired bunches of wheat together into a circle and added the delphiniums between the wheat heads, securing them with wire

form a very compact shape. If the stems of the cereal are firm enough to be inserted in the dry foam without breaking there is no need to wire the stems beforehand. If you do need to wire them, see page 53.

Carry on arranging the wheat from the centre outwards, making sure as you go that the wheat is placed head to head to form a horizontal line at the top of the arrangement. Leave a gap of about three to five centimetres around the rim of the container between the exposed stems of wheat and the actual edge of the bowl.

Take the green reindeer moss (for this arrangement I preferred a darker green moss to create a greater contrast with the blue of the container) and insert it all around the wheat to form a neat border between the wheat and the rim of the container.

Once the wheat is in place, you can use what is left over, as I did, for the extra decoration. Plait full length stems of wheat together, tying the ends with some florist wire, and loop it carefully around the middle of the wheat in the arrangement. Then gather all the ears together to form an enormous pompon, and fix it in the centre of the plait as shown in the photograph. This adds a final touch of originality and breaks up the severity of the arrangement.

Alternatively, you could plait the extra ears of wheat into a wreath shape, and decorate with dried country flowers – a pretty ornament for a plain door.

Laura and Benjamin, the author's two children, helping to prepare and cut the wheat in a field in the south-west of France, for this country arrangement

A MOSS
BEAR

A lovable, charming little teddy bear, approximately 30 × 26 cm (12 × 10 in), made entirely from moss. A moss bear can be modelled on your favourite teddy bear, and is sure to find a place anywhere, in any bear lover's home! The tartan bow around his neck adds a final distinctive touch of character.

As with all dried flowers, do not place the moss bear under direct sunlight as the moss would inevitably lose its green colour very quickly.

MAKING THE MOSS BEAR

This is a fairly challenging project, and takes some patience, but do not be disillusioned. Once you have started making the legs and arms of the bear you will realize that you are more than half-way to completing him, and you will be more than encouraged to finish.

First of all set the teddy bear you wish to copy against a wall, on a stool, so that you have it in front of you at eye level. You must be able to see all its features clearly, without too many shadows getting in the way. Adjust the light in the room where you are working so that you can see where the bear's stomach ends, and the shape of its mouth and eyes. Too much light in the room will erase the important shadows on the bear's body, which you need to capture in the moss. Once you are satisfied with the position of your teddy bear and the lighting, you can start cutting the stub wire into approximately 17 cm (7 in) lengths so that all the wires are ready and to hand. You will need to be able to use them quickly when you find yourself supporting the bear in one hand and using the other hand to insert the wire into the moss, on to the dry foam.

Carpet moss is quite thick, and usually comes from the florist or the flower market in boxes, so you may need to take off some of the soil attached to it. Once laid on the floral foam it will rapidly add volume to the whole bear, so you must judge this carefully as you plan how to cut out the pieces of dry foam.

THE LEGS AND ARMS

Cut four cuboid shapes roughly 18 × 7 cm (7 × 3 in) from the large block of dry foam. Cut one corner of each cuboid at a 45° angle so that the legs and arms will fit well into the main body. Cover the cuboids with some of the carpet moss, following the shape of your model bear, and use your stub wire to secure the moss to the dry foam, bending the wire over to fix the moss in place. The wire must remain hidden inside the dry foam: if it is too long, cut it shorter. Leave the body end of the arms and legs

MATERIALS

One bunch of stub wire
Four or five blocks of dry foam
One ribbon wide enough to form a bow around the bear's neck
A glue gun or other adhesive

FLOWERS AND FOLIAGE

Two boxes of carpet or pin-cushion moss (*Leucobryum glaucum*)
The centre of a *Helipterum roseum* flower or any dried marguerite

THE LOCATION

When a buyer from a major store in London commissioned me to make a character for them in moss, I found my inspiration in my daughter's bedroom, where I discovered her favourite teddy bear. I liked his general appearance and decided to use him as my model. I sat him on a radiator in front of me, and it all began from there. That was my first bear, and I was almost as excited by the results as my children were when they saw my first creation in moss sitting one morning on the breakfast table! Even now, I still use the same teddy bear each time I am asked to make a moss bear for a special occasion.

Moss bears can make the most delightful presents, and can be made to carry some flowers themselves or simply have a lovely bow around their neck. The fresh moss keeps its colour for more than a year, as long as you remember to spray it from time to time with some water to keep the moss moist and green.

A charming moss bear can be displayed almost anywhere in the home, but do remember it is not a children's toy. Moss bears are really ornaments, that will amuse your guests: they add a touch of humour in any interior and set against a bowl of fruit, next to a dish of pot-pourri, or next to a family photograph, this moss bear is truly welcome by the whole family and friends.

(where you have cut your 45° angle) uncovered, to enable you to fit them nicely on to the main body. The moss covering the rest of the body will eventually cover these ends too, and no dry foam will show.

THE BODY

Cut a squarish block from dry foam, judging its size from the actual size of the teddy bear you are using as a model – (this one's body was 23 × 14 cm (9 × 5 in)). *Make it smaller than the actual size of the body of the teddy bear*, because of the volume the moss adds once pinned on the dry foam. Cut the corners of the square block of dry foam at a 45° angle where the arms and legs of the bear will fit into the body. Now pin moss over the body of the bear, following the shape of your model bear. Do not press too hard on the moss when pinning it down, in order to avoid unwanted shadows on the finished bear. Leave gaps where the arms and legs will join the body.

When you are fully satisfied with the shape of the body you can start pinning the limbs of the moss bear to the body, using as much wire as necessary to make the body sturdy enough to be moved around without running the risk of losing a leg on the way! For this purpose, you must use long stub wire so that the legs and arms remain fixed firmly in their required position. I find it best to choose a sitting position, so that the bear can sit comfortably on any flat surface.

When the legs and arms are in place, fill in any gaps at the joins with moss, and add touches of moss to the tummy of the moss bear to make it look as cuddly and rounded as your model teddy bear.

Any shadows you notice on your model bear can easily be simulated on your moss bear by pinning some wire on the required spot. Gradually, as you copy the various lines the light has created on the teddy, your moss bear will take on some of the character of your teddy bear.

A moss bear makes an amusing present and could be made to carry a small bunch of the flowers of your choice

THE HEAD, THE EARS AND THE NOSE

You might think the head is more difficult to make than the rest, but once you have finished the body, arms and legs, you will undoubtedly be encouraged and by now impatient to see the end result of your first creation in moss, so have faith!

Taking your teddy bear as the model for your moss bear, judge the size of its head, and cut out a square block of dry foam – do not forget that the moss will add to its volume. For this bear, cover a 9 × 9 cm (3½ × 3½ in) square block of dry foam with the moss in the same way as before until it resembles a rounded ball. Once it is covered, pin it down on the main body of the moss bear, using long stub wire so that the head is well secured to the body.

At this point the rounded ball of moss will not resemble the head of the teddy bear at all, but do not despair. Use as much wire as necessary to pin the head down on the body of the moss bear. Make sure the wire

does not protrude from the body of the moss bear, which would be both unattractive and dangerous.

When you are satisfied that the head is firmly in place, you can start preparing the ears. For this purpose cut some small triangular pieces of dry foam, no larger than 5 cm in height (2 inches) for the size of the bear featured here. Cover them with moss as before, using very short stub wire. Pin the whole ear on the side of the head, copying the position of the ears on the teddy bear. On the inside of the ear, pin down some short stub wire so that you create a shadow, as if it were the hollow part of the ear. Continue until you are satisfied that your moss bear resembles your teddy bear.

Moving on to the main part of the face, you will notice that the bear has a round, flat nose. Add a small piece of moss roughly at the centre of the bear's face and he will suddenly take on more interesting expressions. Use the centre of a helipterum flower for the nose itself, gluing it down on the moss with your glue gun. Press it lightly and wait for the glue to dry before letting it go.

THE EYES

I do not tend to use any materials for the eyes but prefer working with shadows there too. To that effect, I use some short cut wires and pin them down where the eyes should be. This effect is wonderful, since you will give your bear an expression that is different every time. Your first bear will never look the same as the second one, nor, I am sure, all the others to follow.

If you are having difficulty in making your bear remain seated, just add some more moss to his back until he sits comfortably on a flat surface. The back may seem somewhat straight and long but it does not really matter as it will be counterbalanced by the rather rounded tummy.

For the final touch, take a piece of material that matches the colour of your sitting-room (let us say), make a bow and tie it around the bear's neck. Secure it by using a small-headed pin and pressing it on the moss.

If protected from direct sunlight, as always, your bear should last for more than a year. Spray it with water occasionally to keep the moss fresh and green longer.

Your moss bear will be the delight of your guests, family and children.

Designed by Lynne Lawrence in London, this sculptured moss elephant rests on a balcony. The moss needs only to be sprayed with water from time to time to keep its colour fresh and green

AN ELEGANT SYMMETRICAL DESIGN

An arrangement of red and white roses, 70 × 26 cm (27 × 10 in), for an oak-panelled dining room; the dried, long-stemmed, red and white roses enhance the refinement of this town house. Arranged upright, in a symmetrical style, they add some light in a rather dark dining room, thanks to the highlighting effect of the rows of white roses between the rich red roses that blend with the sumptuous wallpaper.

MATERIALS

One large size bread basket or similar wicker
    basket
Some stub wire
Eight blocks of dry floral foam

FLOWERS AND FOLIAGE

Ten bunches of white roses
Ten bunches of red roses
Fresh green sphagnum moss, enough to cover all
    the exposed sides of the basket

THE LOCATION

I decided on a symmetrical look for this arrangement
because of the extreme elegance of the surroundings. The
18th-century furniture made me decide on white and red
roses for the main flowers, to form a contrast with the
dark background of the furniture. Also, the owner men-
tioned that she liked using fresh flowers in her home but
made an exception for certain rooms where there was
hardly any natural light. White and red roses were
therefore a good choice for the illusion they give of fresh
roses, even when dried.

I bought ten bunches each of fresh white and red roses
and dried them myself (hanging them upside down in a dry
and warm place for about eight days – see page 41). It is
worth drying the roses yourself, since it is very easy, and
dried white roses in particular can be hard to find.
Remember that flowers tend to go darker when they dry:
here I bought light red roses, so that when dried they
acquired the required colour, a deep red.

**Dried, long-stemmed, red and white roses enhance the
refinement found throughout this town house. Arranged in a
symmetrical style, upright, they add some light in a rather grand
but dark dining-room, thanks to the highlighting effect of the
rows of white roses in between the red roses that blend with
the wallpaper**

Most dried flowers, particularly delphiniums, roses, paeonies, lavender, or any cereal, such as wheat, oats or barley, can be arranged symmetrically by placing the flower stems directly in the floral foam, tightly placed against each other, and upright. They can be arranged into any shape, to fit the style and patterns of your room – round, oval, square or rectangular.

This symmetrical style is extremely versatile, and goes well in almost any room of the house, but it needs to be positioned where the arrangement can be seen from the top, since the heads of the flowers are all gathered at the top of the arrangement and not around it. The elegance of a symmetrical design can complement almost any interior, whether it be modern or classically furnished.

THE CONTAINER

I used a large sized, but quite narrow, bread basket, that could fit into any shelf in a dining room, a sitting room or a hall and could be moved around freely. The shape and size of the basket was ideal for the rectangular arrangement I had in mind.

MAKING THE ARRANGEMENT

PREPARING THE CONTAINER

Although the shape of the bread basket was ideal for the shape I wanted for the arrangement, baskets almost inevitably look rustic, and that would have been inappropriate in this particularly elegant town house. So I needed to find a way to hide the basket (but depending on your container and your home, you may not think this necessary). If you want to do the same take some sphagnum moss, which can be obtained from your flower market.

It is always possible to hide unwanted features on a container if necessary: here the basket is the perfect size but the wrong colour for this room, so palm leaves are glued against the sides to disguise it. The fresh green moss that will eventually dry creates an illusion of very pale pink roses growing through mossy earth. A very simple, elegant arrangement, for a simple yet very stylish interior

Cover the outside of the basket by securing the moss on the sides of the basket with stub wire. I left the handles free from moss for practical reasons and to avoid too much heaviness in the general appearance of the container itself.

Once the basket is covered with moss start laying the blocks of dry foam inside it, firmly positioned so that when the basket is moved around the blocks of dry foam stay where they are. To ensure this, use some stub wire to fix the blocks of floral foam to each other so that they form a whole block without any space between them. Then add a thin layer of moss on top of the blocks of floral foam so that the foam does not show.

ARRANGING THE FLOWERS

First divide the roses into two groups, white and red. Then decide on the right length for the stem to suit the container and its size, and cut all the roses to the same length. When arranged, they should form a very straight horizontal line at the top. I wanted my arrangement to be quite high, and so chose very long stemmed roses.

Since I wanted to achieve a very marked symmetrical look I decided to arrange the flowers in layers, or stripes, white roses followed by red roses, putting the roses in one by one, and alternating the colour every so often. Of course, you can create any pattern you like, or keep just to one colour if you prefer.

The stems of these roses were relatively strong because of their size, and I could for the most part stick them into the dry foam without wiring the stems, but always wire a stem if it seems in the least bit fragile (see page 53).

Finally, I glued a few of the rose petals here and there on the moss on the sides of the container. Again, the choice is yours. But such a finishing touch can really lift the arrangement.

A CLASSICAL ARRANGEMENT

A large arrangement, 110 cm high × 88 cm (43 × 35 in), set in a hall leading into a beautiful garden. The dried green foliage reflects the greenery outside, and also acts as a foil for the dramatic colour of the walls. The swags of ruscus around the container are linked by the pale yellow flowers of achillea, the only flower in the arrangement, which echoes perfectly both the strong yellow walls and the gilding on the urn.

A PICTURE

An abstract picture, 63 × 43 cm (25 × 17 in) for an architect's studio. Finding a way to present flowers in a home where the decoration is highly minimalist, and where sparsity and architectural features are the predominant theme, can be difficult. This modern arrangement, set strikingly in an antique frame, breaks the austerity and adds warmth to a very contemporary studio flat, and is the perfect decorative compromise where there is little room or desire for a conventional arrangement.

MATERIALS

A picture frame of any age or style
A piece of ply board, cut to the required shape
    and size for the picture backing
Adhesive – a glue gun is ideal for greater control
A few screws

FLOWERS AND FOLIAGE

Sixteen bunches of *Helianthus* (sunflowers)
Ten bunches of orange tree flowers
One bag of dark green reindeer moss

THE LOCATION

In a very small or very sparse interior, there may not be room for a conventional dried flower arrangement, or it may not seem appropriate. In this modern studio, where architectural elements play the most important part in the decoration scheme, I decided to continue the general theme and chose a very restrained design where geometrical lines would predominate. The best approach, without intruding on an already well-defined style, was to introduce flowers in a picture frame where they would be arranged in a fairly geometrical pattern, to reflect the modern interior. There was also another factor that influenced my choice: from a practical point of view, space is very valuable for architects, who may have plans of their drawings scattered all over the place while working on a project, so it was also more convenient to display the flowers in a picture frame.

THE CONTAINER

In this instance I chose an old, slightly ornate frame to take away a little from the rather stark whiteness of the walls. You can of course use any style of frame in keeping with your room and the flowers of your choice.

MAKING THE ARRANGEMENT

PREPARING THE CONTAINER

Once you have chosen a picture frame to suit your interior, measure its perimeter and cut some ply board to fit inside the actual frame, as if it were a painting. You will be using ply board as the base for the flower arrangement, so make sure it can be removed easily when the need arises; you may want to use screws at each corner of the board to screw on the back of the actual frame without damaging it. If you cannot do this yourself a carpenter will do this for you in no time at all, at very little cost.

ARRANGING THE FLOWERS

Select the flowers for your picture in the same way as you would for a more ordinary arrangement. The choice of colours and textures is crucial here. Do not forget that the picture will probably be hung on a wall, and will therefore be much more obviously part of the decoration, so go for colours and a design that blend well. This particular studio is almost entirely colourless, so I decided on a striking orange theme to make a noticeable splash of colour. I chose some sunflowers and orange tree flowers both for their similar colour tone and markedly circular shape, which were perfect for the geometrical design I wanted, and I used the exquisitely fragranced orange tree flowers for the centre of the picture.

Of course you need not stick to geometrical shapes: you can create all sorts of designs with dried flowers as long as their texture allows you to work with them. If you decide on the same design as the one shown here, start by laying the border and deciding on its width. If you have fewer sunflowers than me, make the border wider. Here I chose a border of 12cm (5in).

Put a few drops of glue (using a glue gun if you have one) around the edge of the ply board, starting from one corner. Then take some reindeer moss, and working your way down the edge of the ply board press it down on to the board where the glue is. Try to create a straight line all round, although it does not really matter since the other flowers and their petals will inevitably disturb the evenness of the outside border.

Use only the heads of the orange tree flowers in the centre of the ply board and glue each one of them very carefully upright on the board as tightly together as

A picture, composed from dried flowers and other materials is a wonderful compromise for someone who has little room or desire for a conventional arrangement, and no time to look after fresh flowers. The curl in the sunflower petals echoes the design in the frame. A dried flower arrangement that truly becomes a work of art

possible, head against head, until you form a circle of the required size. These orange tree flowers are imported from Tunisia and may be quite difficult to find on the market, but you can use any other flowers of interesting shape or texture. Once you are satisfied with the shape of the circle made with the orange tree flowers, cut the sunflowers and just keep the heads. Try to cut the stem as close as possible to the base of the head so that they can be easily glued flat on the board. Fill all the space left between the border and the circle with the heads of the sunflowers by gluing each head individually and pressing it hard on the board, letting it go after a few seconds.

Once the flowers are all glued on the ply board, you can screw the board itself to the back of your frame. Be careful not to damage the frame. Your picture is now ready.

The variety of flowers, colour and designs you can create in this way is endless.

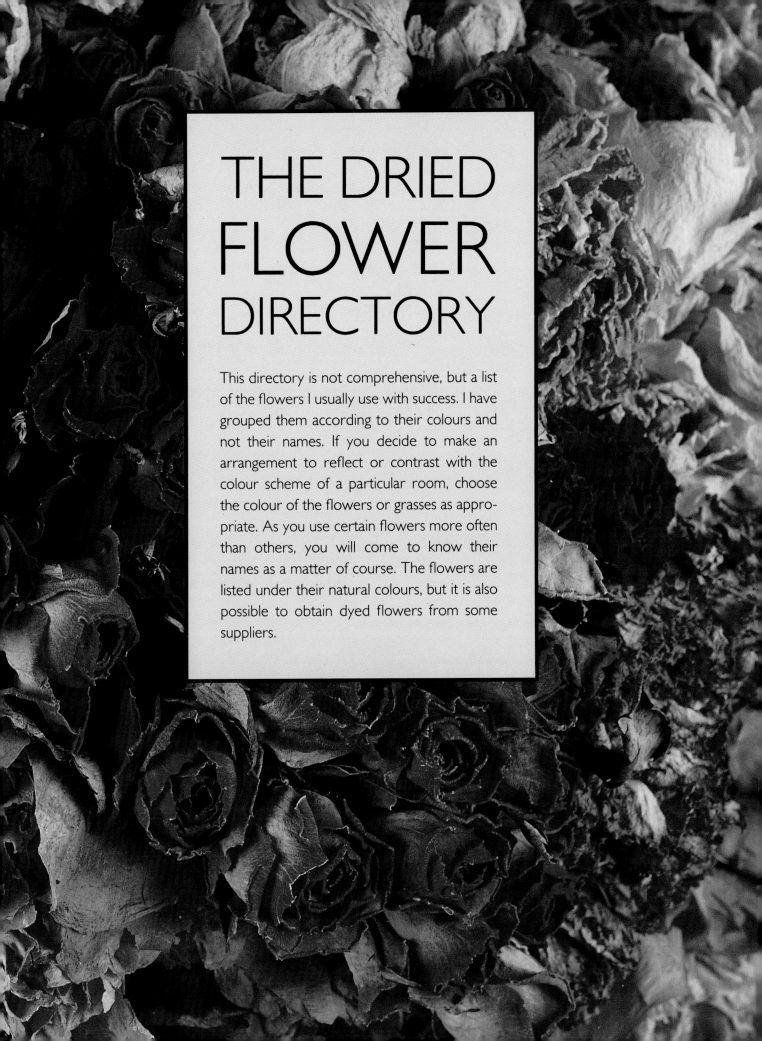

THE DRIED FLOWER DIRECTORY

This directory is not comprehensive, but a list of the flowers I usually use with success. I have grouped them according to their colours and not their names. If you decide to make an arrangement to reflect or contrast with the colour scheme of a particular room, choose the colour of the flowers or grasses as appropriate. As you use certain flowers more often than others, you will come to know their names as a matter of course. The flowers are listed under their natural colours, but it is also possible to obtain dyed flowers from some suppliers.

DEEP PINK
AND PURPLE

Achillea millefolium 'Lilac Beauty' (yarrow)

The heads are ideal for sculptured arrangements

Ageratum

Particularly effective in country or natural style arrangements where the flowers are loosely arranged

Dahlia

Dahlias work particularly well in sculptured arrangements, using just the flower heads, which separate very easily from the stems

Delphinium (larkspur)

Although fragile – you may lose some flowers from the stem when you handle the plant – dried delphiniums evoke the fresh flowers wonderfully and hence are excellent in natural style arrangements. They can also be used in symmetrical displays

Helichrysum bracteatum (strawflower)

Best kept together as a whole bunch. Ideal for creating a natural look

Helipterum roseum (syn. Acroclinium roseum)

The heads separate easily from their stems, and make wonderful sculptured arrangements

Limonium sinuatum (statice, sea lavender)

Handle with care, as this is quite fragile. Most effective when used as a whole bunch, particularly in a natural style arrangement

Paeonia

Beautiful in all styles of arrangement, and can be air dried or dried with silica gel equally successfully

Rosa 'Europa', *R.* 'Gerda', *R.* 'Jacaranda', *R.* 'Joy', *R.* 'Motrea'

Suitable for all styles of arrangement. The flower heads break easily from the stems, but the heads themselves are strong and easy to work with

Xeranthemum annuum (immortelle)

Fragile, so best kept as a whole bunch. Ideal for natural styles because of their resemblance to the fresh flowers

Helichrysum

Delphinium

Rosa 'Gerda'

Limonium sinuatum

Helipterum roseum

Ageratum

Achillea 'Lilac Beauty'

Echinops

Eryngium

Papaver

Echinops

Delphinium

Eryngium

Lavendula

PALE PINK
AND PEACH

Dahlia

See deep pink and purple flowers

Delphinium

See deep pink and purple flowers

Helichrysum bracteatum

See deep pink and purple flowers

Helipterum manglesii, H. roseum

Fragile to handle but very effective if kept together in a whole bunch. The dried flowers look very fresh and natural

Limonium suworowii (pink pokers)

Useful both for natural style and for more rigid, symmetrical arrangements because of their strong, thick stems

Paeonia

See deep pink and purple flowers

Rosa 'Gerda', R. 'Rosario'

See deep pink and purple flowers. *Rosa* 'Rosario' is an extremely pale pink

Rosa 'Dorus Rijkers'

See deep pink and purple flowers. This rose has very small heads and very thin stems. Ideal for rose trees, but the heads must be glued on

Silene (campion)

Best kept together as a whole bunch. Ideal for creating a natural look

Xeranthemum annuum

See deep pink and purple flowers

Rosa 'Rosario'

Helipterum manglesii

Silene

Helichrysum

Paeony

Delphinium

RED AND
BURGUNDY

Astilbe

Easy to work with and suitable for both natural style and symmetrical arrangements

Amaranthus (love-lies-bleeding)

Some of the yellow leaves must be removed in the preparation stage. Suitable for natural style and symmetrical arrangements

Celosia cristata (cockscomb)

The velvety appearance of this extraordinary flower makes it ideal for sculptured arrangements

Callistemon citrinus (red bottlebrush)

Perfect for tall arrangements because of its long stems

Dahlia

See deep pink and purple flowers

Helichrysum bracteatum

See deep pink and purple flowers

Nigella damascena

Can be used loosely in traditional style arrangements, or in sculptures. The heads are hollow, so be gentle or you may squash them

Rosa 'Mercedes', R. 'Jaguar'

See deep pink and purple flowers

BROWN AND RUST

Banksia (Australian honeysuckle)

Very large heads, easy to handle. Beware of the weight on the arrangement. Unusual and effective in sculptured arrangements

Bougainvillea

Several bunches, gathered together in much the same way as the lotus flowers on page 9, add a beautiful finishing touch to an arrangement

Carthamus tinctorius

Spiky, adds depth to an arrangement, and can be used with its greenery as an effective filler

Gypsophila (baby's breath)

Delicate flowers that add volume to an arrangement and can be used for most styles in whole bunches

Leucadendron

Use just the heads for sculptured arrangements

Nelumbo nucifera (lotus seed head)

Very attractive in sculptured arrangements, particularly when mixed with other exotic flowers

Protea (Cape honeysuckle)

Long-stemmed flowers with striking flower heads, which add height to tall arrangements

Protea

Gypsophila

Nelumbo nucifera

Carthamus tinctorius

Banksia

Bougainvillea

Leucadendron

YELLOW AND GOLD

Achillea 'Moonshine'

The stems are not very strong, so for sculptured arrangements the heads must be glued on

Alchemilla mollis (lady's mantle)

Ideal for large arrangements because of the volume the branches create. The dried flowers closely resemble the fresh flowers in appearance

Chrysanthemum

Generally best in natural style arrangements, but the small flower heads can be used successfully in topiary trees

Helichrysum bracteatum

See deep pink and purple flowers. Comes in several shades of yellow

Helianthus (sunflower)

The petals lose much of their natural colour when dried, but the flower heads are particularly good for sculptured arrangements and pictures.

Limonium sinuatum

See deep pink and purple flowers

Lonas inodora

The flower heads are quite hard, so are good for sculptured arrangements, but sorting out all the flower heads is quite time-consuming

Orange tree flowers

These are tiny flowers, best in a sculptured arrangement or in a picture, where all the flower heads show. The scent is quite beautiful. Rare on the market, however

Rosa 'Golden Times', *R.* Champagne

See deep pink and purple flowers

x Solidaster hybridus, x S. luteus

Very easy to work with and ideal for a natural style arrangement

Verticordia (feather flower, golden morrison)

Very compact flowers, ideal for sculptured arrangements

Helianthus

Achillea

Helichrysum

Helichrysum

Helichrysum

WHITE
AND CREAM

Achillea

See yellow and gold flowers

Agonis (white ti-tree)

Ideal for tall arrangements because of its long stems

Anaphalis (pearl everlasting)

Gives a round shape and creates volume. Works particularly well around the rim of large, classical containers

Dahlia

See deep pink and purple flowers

Delphinium

See deep pink and purple flowers

Gypsophila (baby's breath)

See brown and rust flowers

Helipterum manglesii, H. roseum

See pale pink and peach flowers

Ixodia (Australian daisy)

These create volume when kept in whole bunches, and have a good colour tone for classical arrangements. The dried flowers resemble the fresh flowers closely

Limonium sinuatum

See deep pink and purple flowers

Nelumbo nucifera (lotus flower)

The queen of dried flowers! Expensive to buy, but just two or three flowers add an exquisite final touch to an arrangement. The heads can be used in the same way as roses and paeonies, and they make wonderful trees

Silene (campion)

See pale pink and peach flowers

Verticordia brownii (cauliflower morrison)

See yellow and gold flowers

Xeranthemum annuum

See deep pink and purple flowers

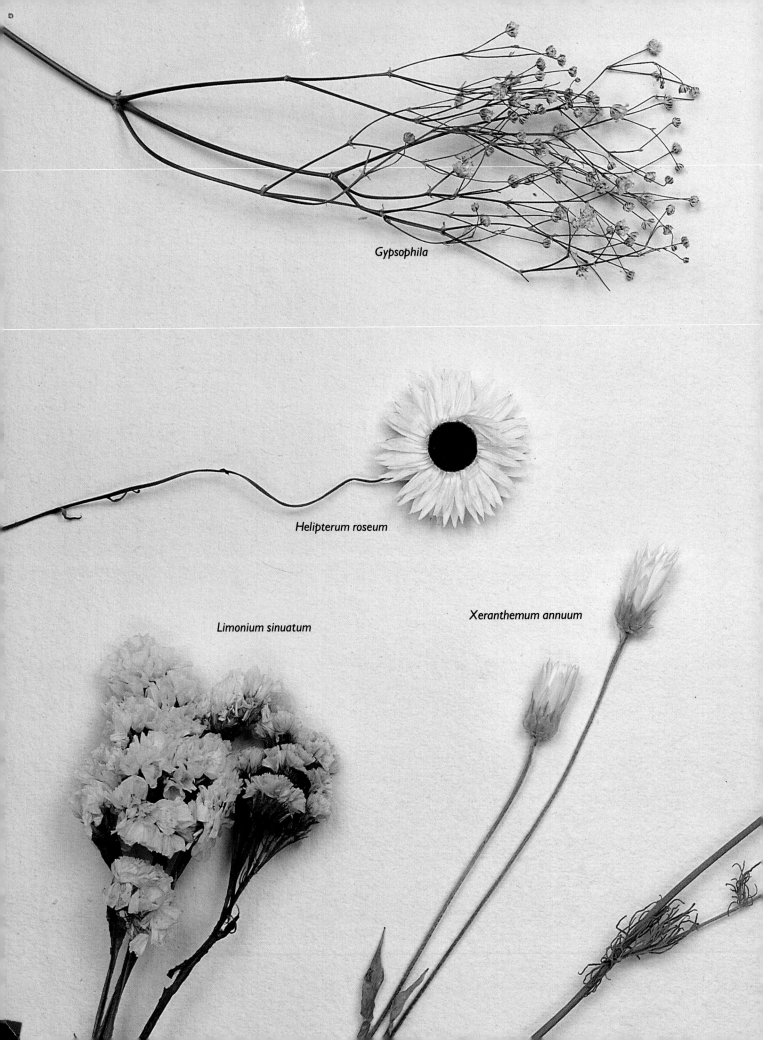

Gypsophila

Helipterum roseum

Limonium sinuatum

Xeranthemum annuum

Helipterum manglesii

Delphinium

Silene

FOLIAGE, SEED HEADS AND CEREALS

Anthurium; magnolia leaves; palm leaves; *Strelitzia* leaves

Leaves of all colours are useful for adding interesting shapes and textures to arrangements

Calytrix (willow myrtle); *Gaultheria shallon* (salal); *Ruscus aculeatus* (butcher's broom); *Quercus ilex* (holly oak)

These types of foliage come in a range of greens and work well used in a spray or in bunches for large arrangements

Amaranthus cordatus 'Viridus' (love-lies-bleeding); *Bupleurum* (shrubby hare's ear); *Carthamus tinctorius* (safflower); *Kunzea*

The foliage is very effective used with the flowers in sprays or bunches

Alyssum; *Echinops* (globe thistle); *Iberis* (candy-tuft); *Nelumbo nucifera* (lotus); *Nigella damescena, N. orientalis* (love-in-a-mist); *Papaver* (poppy)

The seed heads of these flowers all add interest and texture to any style of arrangement

Avena (oat grass); *Briza maxima* (quaking grass); *Bromus* (brome grass); *Hordeum* (barley); *Phalaris* (canary reed grass); *Phleum pratensis* (cat's tail, Timothy grass); *Polypogon* (beard grass); *Setaria* (foxtail grass); *Triticum* (wheat)

Grasses can be used in bunches or in single stems and are useful for many styles of arrangement, particularly to create a country look

Iberis

Alyssum

Hordeum

Briza maxima

Avena

Bromus

Triticum

Avena

Lagurus

Phalaris

FURTHER READING

BARRY, J. Ferguson, and COWAN, Tom, *Living with Flowers*, Rizzoli International Publications, Inc., New York (1990)

BLACK, Penny, *A Passion for Flowers*, Ebury Press, London (1992)

BLACK, Penny, *The Scented House*, Dorling Kindersley, London (1990)

DUFF, Gail, *Natural Fragrances*, Sidgwick & Jackson, London (1989)

HILLIER, Malcolm and HILTON, Colin, *The Complete Book of Dried Flowers*, Dorling Kindersley, London (1986)

HOLM, Aase, *Tage Andersen*, Bergen Forlag, Denmark (1991)

LAWRENCE, Mary, *The Creative Book of Pressed Flowers*, Salamander Books Ltd, London (1988)

MITCHELL, Ann Lindsay, *The Dried Flower Garden*, B.T. Batsford Ltd, London (1990)

NEWDICK, Jane, *Period Flowers, Designs for today*, Charles Letts & Co Ltd, London (1991)

NIESEWAND, Nonie, *Tricia Guild's Natural Flower Arranging*, Mitchell Beazley Publishers, London (1986)

OHRBACH, Barbara, *The Scented Room*, Sidgwick & Jackson, London (1986)

OTIS, Denise, and MAIA, Ronaldo, *Decorating with Flowers*, Harry N. Abrams, Inc. Publishers, New York (1978)

PETELIN, Carol, *The Country Diary Book of Flowers*, Webb & Bower, London (1991)

PULBROOK and GOULD, *Flowers for Special Occasions*, B.T. Batsford Ltd, London (1982)

PULLEYN, Rob, *The Wreath Book*, Sterling Publishing Co, Inc., New York (1988)

RADCLIFFE, Barbara Rogers, *Drying Flowers*, Merehurst Ltd, London (1992)

RADCLIFFE, Barbara Rogers, *Making Wreaths and Garlands*, Merehurst Ltd, London (1992)

TONKS, Diana, *Spectacular Flowers*, B.T. Batsford Ltd, London (1991)

TURNER, Kenneth, *Flower Style*, Weidenfeld & Nicolson, London (1989)

VAGG, Daphne, *The Flower Arrangers A–Z*, B.T. Batsford Ltd, London (1989)

WESTLAND, Pamela, *Arranging Flowers Naturally*, Quintet Publishing Ltd, London (1991)

WESTLAND, Pamela, *Decorating With Dried Flowers*, Quintet Publishing Ltd, London (1991)

SUPPLIERS

Dried flowers are becoming more and more widely available. You can either buy them directly or ask for mail order catalogues from some of the bigger suppliers: your local florist should be able to advise you.

Your florist may or may not stock an extensive supply of dried flowers, but other sources include flower markets, garden centres, nurseries, department stores and furnishing stores – in fact, almost anywhere you can find fresh flowers, and other places besides!

For more information about Star Flowers, who kindly supplied many of the flowers for the arrangements in this book, and for a copy of their catalogue, please write to:

Star Dried Flowers B.V.
Floralaan 2a
P.O. Box 101
2230 AC Rijnsburg
Holland

Britannia Nurseries, who as one of Star Flowers' British outlets also helped with the book, is based at:

Bryanstone Road
off Eleanor Cross Road
Waltham Cross
Hertfordshire
EN8 7NS

INDEX